GREEK MYTHS

THE BATTLE OF THE OLYMPIANS AND THE TITANS

A RETELLING BY
CARI MEISTER

ILLUSTRATED BY
RICH PELLEGRINO

PICTURE WINDOW BOOKS
a capstone imprint

CAST OF CHARACTERS

TITANS (TY-TENZ): giant children of Gaia and Uranus

GAIA (GUY-UH): Mother Earth, married to Uranus; mother of the Titans, the Hundred-Handed Ones, and the Cyclopes

URANUS (YUH-RAY-NUHS): The Sky, married to Gaia; father of the Titans, the Cyclopes, and the Hundred-Handed Ones

CRONUS (KROH-NUHS): son of Gaia and Uranus; Titan ruler

CYCLOPES (SY-KLOPS): sons of Gaia and Uranus; one-eyed giants

HUNDRED-HANDED ONES: the three sons of Gaia and Uranus who each have 50 heads and 100 arms

RHEA (REE-UH): Titan daughter of Gaia and Uranus and wife of Cronus

ZEUS (ZOOS): son of Rhea and Cronus; Olympian god of sky, and ruler of mankind

AMALTHEIA (AM-AL-THEE-UH): fairy goat that raises Zeus

HADES (HAY-DEEZ): son of Rhea and Cronus; Olympian god of the Underworld

POSEIDON (PUH-SY-DUHN): son of Rhea and Cronus; Olympian god of the sea

HESTIA (HES-TEE-UH): daughter of Rhea and Cronus; Olympian goddess of the hearth

DEMETER (DIH-MEE-TUR): daughter of Rhea and Cronus; Olympian goddess of agriculture

HERA (HIR-UH): daughter of Rhea and Cronus, and wife of Zeus; Olympian goddess of marriage and the family

OLYMPIANS (OH-LIHM-PEE-ENZ): gods led by Zeus who ruled from Mount Olympus

WORDS TO KNOW

MOUNT OLYMPUS—home of the Olympian gods

MOUNT OTHRYS—battle headquarters for the Titans

MYTHICAL—occurring in myths, or stories from ancient times

TARTARUS—deepest, darkest pits on Earth

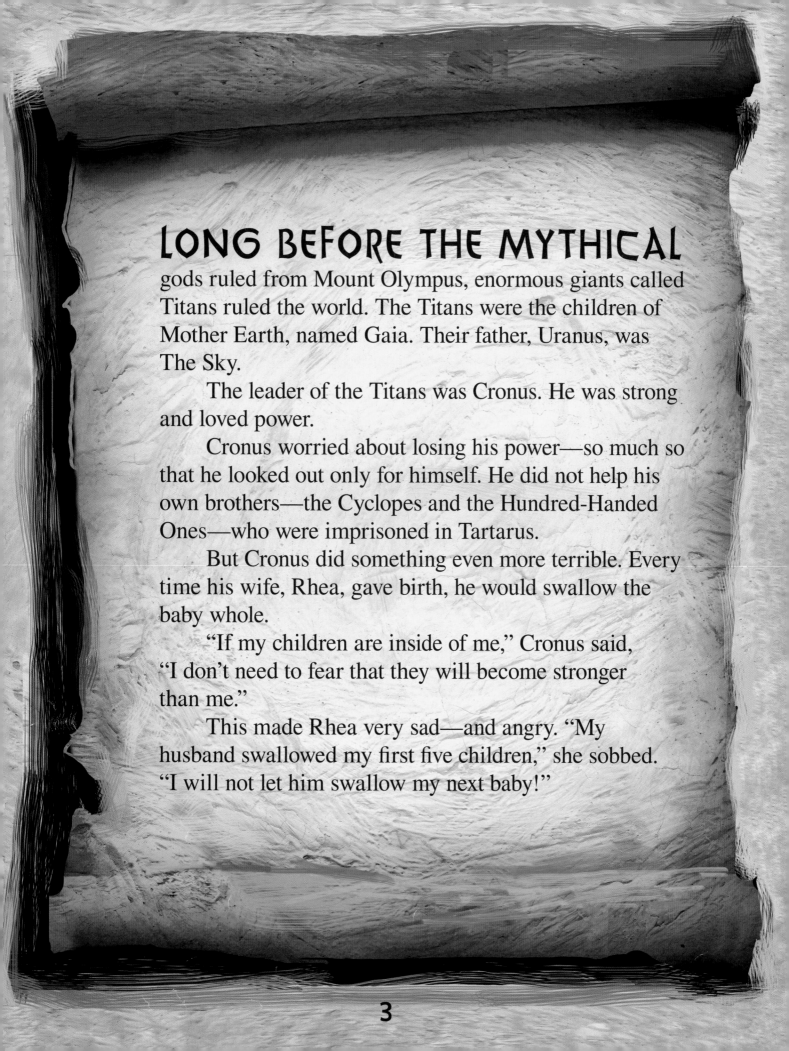

LONG BEFORE THE MYTHICAL

gods ruled from Mount Olympus, enormous giants called Titans ruled the world. The Titans were the children of Mother Earth, named Gaia. Their father, Uranus, was The Sky.

The leader of the Titans was Cronus. He was strong and loved power.

Cronus worried about losing his power—so much so that he looked out only for himself. He did not help his own brothers—the Cyclopes and the Hundred-Handed Ones—who were imprisoned in Tartarus.

But Cronus did something even more terrible. Every time his wife, Rhea, gave birth, he would swallow the baby whole.

"If my children are inside of me," Cronus said, "I don't need to fear that they will become stronger than me."

This made Rhea very sad—and angry. "My husband swallowed my first five children," she sobbed. "I will not let him swallow my next baby!"

Rhea came up with a plan. When baby Zeus was born, she wrapped up a rock in baby linens and presented it to Cronus. "Here is our baby," she said.

Cronus grunted, took the disguised rock, and swallowed it whole.

Rhea secretly rejoiced. "I've fooled him!" she thought.

That night as Cronus slumbered, Rhea took baby Zeus to the secret island of Crete.

"My sweet baby Zeus," Rhea said, "don't worry. I'm putting you in Amaltheia's care. She will give you everything you need. Someday when the time is right, Amaltheia will tell you about your father. Then you will seek revenge."

Amaltheia, a fairy goat, nursed Zeus and taught him many things. In time, Zeus grew into a strong, young god.

8

When Zeus was 15 years old, Amaltheia told him that his father had swallowed his brothers and sisters.

Zeus was furious! "How could anyone do such a thing?" he thundered.

Immediately he set out to seek revenge. On his way, he picked a magic herb. "With this magic herb," he said, "I will trick my father into coughing up my brothers and sisters."

It did not take long for Zeus to find Cronus. After all, Cronus was huge. His odor was so strong, you could smell him from hundreds of miles away.

"Mighty god," Zeus said as he approached his father, "I come from the island of Crete. There we grow magic herbs. Take this and eat it. The herb will make you the most powerful god of all time."

"Give it to me, you fool!" Cronus said.

Cronus wolfed down the herb. "Ha!" he said. "No one will ever take my power now!"

Zeus watched Cronus turn green and then purple. Soon a horrible gurgling noise filled the air.

Cronus coughed, and out flew the rock in baby linens. He coughed again, and out popped his first five children: Hades, Poseidon, Hestia, Demeter, and Hera.

"Thank you, brother!" they said to Zeus. Then they all turned to face their father.

Cronus was returning to his normal color. When he saw his children, he quickly ran to Mount Othrys to gather up a Titan army.

At Mount Othrys, Cronus made a speech. "My fellow Titans!" he said. "We must go to war. My children are angry with me. They seek to remove me from my throne. They will send you to the deepest, darkest pits of Tartarus."

High up on Mount Olympus, Zeus also prepared for war. "My brothers and sisters!" he said. "You have spent your lives inside the belly of our ravenous father. It is time for revenge! Help me defeat the Titans, and together we Olympians shall rule!"

Just then the ground shook. The Titans attacked. They stomped their giant feet, sending more earthquakes throughout the lands.

"Keep steady!" Zeus commanded.

When the earthquakes ceased, Zeus and the other gods of Olympus readied their bows. The first arrows shot out toward the Titans. The battle had begun!

The Olympians were smarter, but the Titans were much larger. Wit clashed against brute force.

The earth shook. Mountains fell. A deep crevice formed when an injured Titan dragged his leg behind him back to Mount Othrys.

The battle wore on. Weeks passed, then months, and then years.

After years of fighting on land, Zeus issued a new battle cry. "To the sea!" he yelled. "Perhaps we can defeat the Titans in the water!"

The Olympians hit the water first. Cronus was not far behind. He took a huge breath and blew. A colossal wave rolled toward the Olympians.

"Watch out!" yelled Zeus.

"Quickly," said Hera, "Put our shields together. We can make a raft!"

A few minutes later, a red-haired Titan trapped Demeter underwater.

"Look here, ugly beast!" Zeus cried. The Titan turned to face him. Zeus held up a giant shield. The sun's reflection hit the Titan in the eyes.

"You're blinding me!" he yelled.

It was enough of a distraction that Hera was able to free Demeter.

18

The war dragged on and on—sometimes on land and sometimes at sea. Some days the Titans seemed to be winning. At other times, the Olympians seemed to have the upper hand.

One day, as mountains were crashing down around him, Zeus made a very wise move.

"Hades!" he said. "I have an idea. I will be back—with strong reinforcements."

Hades strained to stay alive as his brother went down to Tartarus.

Tartarus was dark, wet, and cold. "If I can find my uncles and free them, I am sure they will fight on our side," Zeus thought.

Then he saw them—the Cyclopes and the Hundred-Handed Ones. They were trapped behind thick prison bars.

"Uncles!" he said. "I am your nephew Zeus. Your own brother—my father—will not free you. If you agree to fight on my side, *I* will free you!"

"We will fight with you, Zeus!" said the Hundred-Handed Ones. "We can throw rocks better than anyone else."

"We can make the strongest weapons," said the Cyclopes. "We will fight with you too!"

A guard came near, so Zeus crept into the shadows and hid. As soon as the guard fell asleep, Zeus grabbed the key and set his uncles free.

The Cyclopes went right to work. They were excellent blacksmiths. The night sky lit up with sparks from their hammers as they forged strong swords and shields.

"We also made three special gifts," said the Cyclopes.

"For Hades we made a magical helmet. It makes the wearer invisible. For Poseidon we made a three-pointed trident. It holds so much power that it will shake the earth and churn the seas. For you, Zeus, we forged powerful thunderbolts. With these thunderbolts, no one will stand in your way."

Zeus thanked the Cyclopes for their gifts. "With these new weapons, we will surely defeat the Titans!" he said.

That night on Mount Olympus, the Olympians plotted their final attack.

Before the morning sun came up, Zeus woke his brother. "Hades," he said. "It is time!"

Hades looked at the magical helmet beside his bed. "I hope it works!" he said, putting the heavy helmet on his head.

"I don't see you," said Zeus. "It must work. Where are you?"

But Hades was already on his way to Mount Othrys.

Soon, Hades was walking among the Titans. "I can't believe how easy this is!" he thought as he quietly gathered up all of their weapons.

Hades ran down the mountain with the weapons. The Olympians, the Cyclopes, and the Hundred-Handed Ones were hiding in the trees. Hades removed his helmet when he saw them, and they ran to meet him.

"Good work!" said Poseidon, shaking his trident. "Now it is our turn!"

The Olympians charged up the mountainside and pushed through Cronus' door.

"Now!" commanded Zeus.

The Hundred-Handed Ones hurled rocks at the Titan army, while Zeus and Poseidon teamed up to face their father.

"Father, you will soon be defeated!" yelled Poseidon as he struck the ground with his powerful trident.

The ground shook so violently that Cronus lost his balance. Zeus knew he had to be quick. In a fury, he threw a blazing thunderbolt at Cronus' feet.

Cronus jumped back in surprise. In that moment, he realized his power was lost. "I'm doomed!" he said as he fled down the mountainside.

Without their leader and weapons, the Titan army was powerless.

The war was over. The Olympians were triumphant! They celebrated with a marvelous feast atop Mount Olympus.

Zeus sent the Titans to the deepest pits of Tartarus.

As for the Olympians, the Cyclopes built them a golden palace on top of Mount Olympus, where the wind never blows, the sun always shines, and the food is plentiful and sweet.

READ MORE

Kimmel, Eric A. *The McElderry Book of Greek Myths.* New York: M. K. McElderry Books, 2008.

O'Connor, George. *Zeus: King of the Gods.* Olympians; 1. New York: First Second, 2010.

Smith, Charles R., Jr. *The Mighty 12: Superheroes of Greek Myth.* New York: Little, Brown, 2008.

INTERNET SITES

FactHound offers a safe, fun way to find Internet sites related to this book. All of the sites on FactHound have been researched by our staff.

Here's all you do:

Visit *www.facthound.com*

Type in this code: 9781404866676

Check out projects, games and lots more at
www.capstonekids.com

LOOK FOR ALL THE BOOKS IN THE GREEK MYTHS SERIES:

THE BATTLE OF THE OLYMPIANS AND THE TITANS

JASON AND THE ARGONAUTS

MEDUSA'S STONY STARE

ODYSSEUS AND THE CYCLOPS

PANDORA'S VASE

THE WOODEN HORSE OF TROY

Thanks to our adviser for his expertise and advice:
Terry Flaherty, PhD
Professor of English
Minnesota State University, Mankato

Editor: Shelly Lyons
Designer: Alison Thiele
Art Director: Nathan Gassman
Production Specialist: Sarah Bennett
The illustrations in this book were created with watercolors, gouache, acrylics, and digitally.

Picture Window Books
1710 Roe Crest Drive
North Mankato, MN 56003
www.capstonepub.com

Library of Congress Cataloging-in-Publication Data
Meister, Cari.
  The battle of the Olympians and the Titans : a retelling / by Cari Meister; illustrated by Rich Pellegrino.
     p. cm. — (Greek myths)
  Includes index.
  ISBN 978-1-4048-6667-6 (library binding)
  1. Gods, Greek—Juvenile literature. 2. Goddesses, Greek—Juvenile literature. 3. Mythology, Greek—Juvenile literature. 4. Titans (Mythology)—Juvenile literature. I. Title. II. Series.

BL783.M45 2012
398.20938'01—dc22   2011006586

Printed in the United States of America in North Mankato, Minnesota.
122011   006506R